Chapter 1

Why do You write?

Okay, so you're interested in this idea of writing. One thing you may want to think about is why do you write? Knowing your purpose is the first step to becoming productive. The reason that I write is to express emotion. I write to try to understand the reality that I'm in. I write because it relieves stress. I write because I have a voice. On this piece of paper, I can say anything I want. You may disagree with some of it and that's okay. That's the beauty of art. It's subjective. So, why do you write? What you want to tell people through your own stories. Maybe you don't write stories maybe you write political articles. You give your opinion on a certain news story hoping that people with you. You may also try to persuade people. That's a reason to write too. Maybe your journalist reporting on the news. Your goal would be to make sure that everyone knows about the story. Maybe you're an author nonfiction and you want to educate people on your topic. Do you see how knowing your purpose makes you more productive? Now you know exactly what you're doing. You may not know how to start but that's okay that's why you're reading this. Whether you're writing an essay for homework or manuscript you will become the new book. Knowing your purpose makes you more productive.

Because this book exists I decided to have a copyright page.

Introduction

Hello, if you're picking up this book and you must be a young writer! Yay, welcome. I wrote this book so that new writers could find an easy get started guide. Please note that this may not have every tip to creative writing that there is. But I hope it helps you get started.

Being a beginning writer myself and a very busy one at that. I wanted to create something like a quick reference guide for new writers. Maybe there are some tips you haven't seen before.

These tips come from my own experience and some tricks that I use personally when writing.

Chapter 2

Do you have the right?

What does it take to call yourself a writer? For me, there are three requirements.

Requirement one: is that you love to read. You can't write books, articles, essays, or poetry unless you read. If you don't enjoy reading a book how are you going to enjoy creating one?

Requirement two: is that you have thoughts. You have to write about something. You have to have an idea.

Requirement three: this is the most important one. Requirement three is that you write. If you write your writer period.

It doesn't matter what you write, just that you write. So if you love writing and want to call yourself a writer, not an aspiring writer. Then go ahead, you have the right to call yourself a writer.

So this was just to give you a little bit of confidence boost. Be proud of yourself, you're a writer.

Chapter 3

Gaining book ideas

Okay so now you're a confident new writer, let's talk about gaining writing ideas. When your very first questions might be: "Where do I start?" Which is fine. Here's one thing that you can hear me say over and over again in this book read a lot. Reading helps you to learn as a writer and inspires you. Reading helps the fresh ideas flow. But the truth is, you need a lot of inspiration to start writing a book. Here are a few tips to help you get that inspiration. First of all, see what type of books you like. Ask yourself why you like them. Could you answer the question, "what's your favorite genre?" Who are some of your favorite authors? Why do you like them? Inspiration will and can be taken from other places too. Maybe music inspires you if so try to look at your favorite songs and artist for your inspiration. Where most of your favorite songs about? Is there a reason for this ongoing theme?

Some listen to comedy or watch TV shows for their inspiration. What's something going on in the news? Do any new story surprising make you think? Was your favorite TV show and why? A writer must look for inspiration everything.

By everything, I also mean nature. For some people, nature is really inspirational. Take a walk outside, try to pay attention to everything, from the sound of the birds to small grass. You probably find some inspiration.

Some people depends on what time they write. Some get inspired late at night. Others like to write their best material at the end of the day.

I've also found that with me, talking about my writing projects or ideas with my friends really help. We can bat ideas off each other.

Sometimes they think of things I never really thought of. Maybe at a different point of view to something.

Sometimes reading out of genre can help too. So don't only read your favorite genres. Try something new you may be inspired by it.

Also, the most important inspiration always comes from yourself. Writers tend to base characters and events in the story of their own life or the way they see reality. So use your voice. Talk about something you care about. Base characters off of different sides of you. We all have more than one face. That's good or bad depending on how you look at it.

Also look at the people around you. Maybe you want to base a character off of your best friend, go for it. Or maybe there's someone who makes a good antagonist?

Inspiration can come from internal struggle as well. Maybe the antagonist is your emotions.

The whole point of this chapter is to have you look deeply into your life for inspiration. The truth is you can find inspiration anywhere if you really try. So as you going about your daily life, try to hold a pad close to you. That way when the inspiration pops, you're ready. Don't let anything go to waste describe everything and learn from everyone.

So for your very first exercise, I want you to grab a pad and anything interesting that happens right down. It could be anything from the morning news to a school drama. This is your own private journal so don't be afraid to write down secrets either. I would like you to do this for about a week. Then take the events of your life that happened over that week and write it into a short story. Do the best you can, you're learning.

Chapter 4

The pre-writing process

Okay, so now you have the confidence to call yourself a writer and you know your purpose. To make things even better you even after first writing idea. Hold on, there are a few steps you must take before ever picking up a pen or I guess nowadays typing. First take a minute and think about your idea. What if it best as a story? Maybe a poem? Or is an essay the perfect fit? Take a moment think about what you want to write.

Next, do your research. Read up on the top of your writing. For example, this whole guide is about writing tips so, if you were to look at my desk now I have about three books all on writing that I'm reading from and taking notes. A good idea is to always carry a journal with you. I personally carry two in my backpack. Write down your writing idea. Try to fledge out as much as you can. Maybe you already of the idea for title or character write it down. Next, try to read as many books as possible on your topic. Let's say you want to write a fantasy book you're not really sure of where you want the plot to go. Then try to read as many fantasy books possible.

I would say try read three series by three different authors. Try to ask what if questions; like what if this happened to my character? What if my character did this? Try to pay attention to the voice and the viewpoint of the stories. What series by which author did you like best? Why? Maybe the author had a really strong voice. Or really maybe really relatable characters. Next, try to think about what viewpoint you want your story to be in. Maybe read the three different series and they each had a different viewpoint. What viewpoint did you like best and why? If you're planning for your main character is going to be involved in all the scenes of your story, then the first-person viewpoint might be easiest. Maybe you want the audience to look at your characters from an outside point of view. If that's true, one of the third person points of view might work for you. Now before you go any further you need characters. Yay! We've made it to my favorite part of the writing pre-writing process. Which is character creation.

Chapter 5

Character creation

Okay so, this chapter we will be discussing character creation. I am one method that I think is very easy to do and it really helps you to fully fledge out your character for your own personal story. It's basically creating a character biography. Let's take an example of one of my own original characters. His name is Seth Rollen. He located in a story called The end of Silence. Which so far it's just a rough draft story sitting on my computer. So let's see how I created the character of Seth. First, think about what purposes you want your characters to serve. Think about what the story's about. The end of silence is a story about a rock band trying to make in the music industry. Seth is the lead singer. I also thought about whatever rock band I wanted. Now with all this in mind, I went with this biography layout. Let's fill Seth's biography out together.

Name: Seth Rollen (A good tip for finding names even though it might be a bit strange, is to go to naming website. (These tend to be baby naming websites) to the name that you like based on character gender. There are some names that fit both genders as well.

Age: 19 (When thinking about character age, think about what age they might need to be to make your story believable. Also, think about what age you like working with most. A lot of my characters tend to be in their late teens or early 20s. If you're writing a children's book you may want to go with younger characters.

Gender: Male (For this one, just think about what gender you like the character to be. You should already know that for writing the biography.

Looks: You can make the looks section as broad as you want. I usually do eye color, if I need to I'll do hair. And if my character is a certain race I may do skin tone. Make this section as long as you need to fully fledge your character's physical appearance. (This is where you want to start thinking about what your character looks like. You may already have an idea in your head. If you need more help a good thing to do would be to Google search a picture of a guy or girl that looks like your character. For Seth, I looked up pictures of guys with black hair. You don't have to find an exact picture of your character. It's just to help you get an idea of what your character may look like in the world. This works for characters who aren't human too. If your character is a dog you may want to look at dog breeds. You get my point.

Personality: (This is again, where you want to think about the purpose of your character. You may want to try to name the first few words that come to mind when you think about your character. You can always expand it if needed later.)

Past : This is where you want to think about your character past. This may take some time to do. Try to pull from your own experiences or maybe the experiences of people around you. Don't try to make their past perfect, it doesn't have to be. If the character believes a certain thing, (for example doesn't believe in love) you may want to use the past explained that.

Now if you still need to get to know your character, then it's time for fun questions. Here are some examples of a few:

What kind of music which a character like?

If your character was at your school, how would he or she act?

What type of clothes is your character wear? (Another fun part of this biography is that you have to go fashion shopping for your character. Think about the close they wear)

Another tip for character creation is to give your character a certain flaw. It doesn't have to be a fatal flaw. Just something to make them imperfect, different, and human. Think about your character's fears. Remember, if you give them something like a fear you have to be able to explain it. Maybe one for the character is that they have low self-esteem. Why? Did something happen in their past? Explain it.

Maybe your character curses a lot. Why? Does it have something to do with their beliefs or lack of? You'll want to think about these things when creating characters.

Also, think about your characters likes and dislikes. Does he or she have a favorite food? Does he or she get annoyed by something? Thinking about these things will enable you to create a more human character.

Basically, just brainstorm all kinds of questions you have about your character, write them into biography. This method quickly helps me to fully fledge out character. It's the easiest way I know to write a character.

You may want to do this for each character in the story. Especially the main ones. You may not have to do it for the minor ones. Remember, characters are like your actors. They help your story come alive, so, it's a good idea to make them feel alive too.

As you're writing your story, is a good idea to keep coming back to your character biographies and updating them as needed. Maybe you needed time to figure out where the character was going to go. Now you know the personality, so updated it would be good. You want to try to get your biographies as detailed as possible. The more detail you get the easier it will be to write your character into the story.

So, copy the biography layout and have fun writing and brainstorming your own characters.

Exercises

Think about one character that you really love. Come up with a biography for that character.

A lot of writers base characters on different parts of themselves. Think about something you really love or hate. Or just something you really want in life. Base a character off of that.

Have you a favorite celebrity? Try to read their biographies look up interviews. How did the past lead to what they're doing now? Learn how you can make your character's life add up

Chapter 6

Hooks

Okay so, now you've done your research and some characters. Did you take the time to get to know your characters? Good! If you didn't finish something, then go back to previous chapters and follow the tips. Cause, guess what? We're building from here.

Okay, so now you probably want to start your first draft. I'll let you. Let's talk about hooks. You know what is; that first sentence that really draws the reader in. The truth is hooked and is scary; because until you write an opening, you're staring at a blank page. Don't pressure yourself too much. First drafts are never meant to be great. They're just for putting the idea down and then editing later. Writers are known to write three or four drafts of one book.

So, hooks, where do we start? Well, let's the thing that a good hook should have; the hook should the distinctive voice of the characters/characters. Think about what you view point or points of view. (We will talk points of view more in depth in the next character). You should at least though have an idea of what point of view and how many points of view you want to use.

Next, you need to hint at the plot.

So, What I would do is... think about your character and your setting. You want your opening sentence to be pretty close the initial action. (The action that sets the story off). Here's the opening line from a book of one of my favorite series, <u>The Warrior Cats</u>: by Erin Hunter. *"It was very dark. Rusty could sense something was near. The young tomcat's eyes opened wide as he scanned the dense undergrowth."*

See? This one actually took a few sentences. The opening paragraph continues to introduce us to the main setting as well as the main character. You don't have to put your whole opening into one sentence. Slow down and build a good opening paragraph. Make sure you remember to build up momentum. Make sure you tell us the setting and also again, make sure that the point of view is very clear. Also, make sure you hint at the plot. Now, you might be asking: how did my example line hint at plot? Well, Rusty is going into the forest; where he later meets Bluestar. If you were to continue to read the story. Also, Rusty meeting Bluestar and is the initial action. So, this opening works great.

Exercises

Recently your favorite book titles. What are the opening lines? How do they lean into the rest of story? Read at least three of your favorite books. Compare the openings. Which one did you like the best and why?

It's time to write the first opening paragraph to your first draft. Think about setting, characters and the point of view you want to go by. Then write at least three opening paragraphs. You can play the point of view if you want. So if you can't decide a point of view may write one paragraph the first person and one paragraph in the third person. Choose which opening you at the best for your draft. Have fun writing your opening paragraph.

Chapter 7

Let's talk points of view

Okay, so I said we would talk about point of view. The truth is, it's a good idea to have the point of view you want to use already in your head before you start writing the first draft. But the truth is, sometimes you want to play the point of view. Or maybe you want to have a book or multiple points of view. How do you decide? Well, the most popular point of view to have in fiction is the two third person points of view. But honestly, depends on how many characters are in your story and if your main character is involved in every scene. If your main characters involved in every scene you could probably go with the first person point of view. If you want your story from a more outside point of view. Third person limited might be the best for you. If you have multiple main characters and they all have an equal purpose in the story. And you want to share their thoughts with the readers, then you would go with third person omniscient. The second person is not really a popular point of view for novels. It can get confusing to read and write. However, if you want your reader to be your main character this might be a point of view worth researching. I just don't have any tips on it because I've never written anything in the second person before.   Another question might be how do you write a book and multiple points of view? My advice would be read a lot of books with multiple points of view. Then choose the two points of view you want to go by. It can be the same point of view for both characters like both in the first person. Or you can let one character have a different point of view than the other. Make sure you write their name at the top of the chapter so that the readers know whose point of view they're in. And make sure both characters have very different defined voices. This is very important if you're going to a story with multiple points of view. Also, another point of advice keep the points of view limited. You don't want to do a book with five different points of view, that's too confusing.   So try to get comfortable with your main character.

Write at least three different openings. Remember that is this is your first draft it doesn't have to be the best thing ever. Once you've written the three different openings choose one that you like and start the rough draft with that opening.

Exercises

Read three different books, what point of view did you like best? What book do you think had the best opening? Why?

How do you think the story will be changed when put from a different characters point of view? Write about it.

Take your life story (your birth) come up with an opening and write it.

Take your favorite character out of the ones you created, (they do not have to be the main character) write an opening from their point of view. How is the story changed?

Chapter 8

Voice

Okay, so we've been talking a lot about voice over the last few chapters. But you may have one question, what is the voice? In writing, the voice can be very hard to describe. In a first-person novel, I would describe it as the feel of the main character. Not just the way he or she talks, but also the way they act, think, and respond to the world around them. And a third person novel you could describe voice as the feel that world. So how do you write good voice?   The truth is, voice happens completely on its own. So in order to perfect your voice, you must write a lot. When writing your opening you probably already found a little bit of your voice, run with it. Also, try to read favorite authors and see what is unique about their voice. What makes each book so different?   Writing is something that takes a long time to perfect. If this still sounds overwhelming to you; then take a minute and think about your story. Think about your main character. Think about what you want to say in the story. This will help you find your voice. Then just start writing, see where it goes. It may also be a good idea to read other writers craft books. Do lots of studying and research. As a writer, it's important that you keep on learning. So yeah, for voice the homework is just to read a lot and write a lot. Pay attention to the way you process and understand things this affects your voice.

Exercises

Try reading different books by the same author. How is the voice similar? How is it different? If it is...

Write about something you like just a quick prompt, something to get you going. Read it over, how does your writing sound unique? How do you think you can improve on it?

Do you have a friend who writes? You really should... Try to read some of their work how is different from yours? What's unique about their writing?

Chapter 9

Productivity

Okay so now you're starting your rough draft. And the truth is probably starting to look like a daunting task. Let's talk productivity.

First, and foremost, there is no time limit. So don't try to unnecessarily rush through anything. Then try to work out a writing schedule that works best for you. I tend to write late afternoons and mostly on weekends when I'm off. Find something that works for you. Now one of the questions you may have is: how do I juggle writing with school? Or work? Maybe even both... Juggling stuff can be hard, especially when writing sometimes take a long time. Start small make time to just write a little bit each day even if it's only 300 words or so. If you have homework do your homework first writing can always be said for a free time, like weekends. Also don't pressure yourself too much. Try not to set unrealistic time goals. While it is helpful to plan out your project. Don't stress yourself out too much about it. You don't have any time limits. You'll publish when you're ready. If you stress out too much, you may find yourself procrastinating and not working on a project at all. Also, read lots of books in the genre that you're working in to keep the ideas flowing. Also, self-care is important to remember to get enough sleep and really care for yourself. Go out and hang out with friends. It's not good if you get too isolated.

What personally helps me is setting weekly writing goals, like maybe 1000 or 2000 words a week. This way, I get the project done in a timely manner without stressing on too much about it. My reward is seeing the growing number of pages on my computer and knowing I'm finishing the story that I started. Another good productivity tip that I heard is to use a timer while writing so that you don't get distracted and you could finish the project quickly.

Also find someone to read your writing. Praise and criticism help me to stay focused on the project. Also writing partners can give you tips on your writings. It's very important to have a writing partner or a beta reader to help you focus on your jobs and even edit them after you are done.

Last productivity tip I want to give you that I think would really help your writing productivity, is to make sure you love what you're writing. You should write for yourself. If another audience likes it that's great but if you're writing with the target audience in mind that you can't relate to you lose interest in your project. And who could blame you? You were never interested in the first place. If you find you having trouble being productive because you don't know when stories going and maybe it's time to step back and plan a little bit more. Before I start a story I have a good idea of the plot already in my head so I don't really feel the need to outline. But some people do an outline and do a lot of preplanning. I find that doing character biographies helps me plan the story as well. Also continually reading genres that are related to my story. If I'm writing a romance, I read a lot of romance books. So maybe would be a good idea for you to outline the scene until you know where it's going. Or gets a character by updating their biography. Or get inspired by reading a book in the library. Different things work for different people.

Exercises

Try to write at different times during the day. What time of day works best for you?

Find out what you need to stay motivated. Are you a person that works on rewards or praise?

Finally look back at your preplanning. If they're any questions you have about a particular part of the story. Then go back to your research and plan the story out further.

Chapter 10

Staying focused

Okay so just talk about productivity, right? But the truth is sometimes staying productive isn't the hard part. Sometimes the hard part is sticking to the original idea of the story. So what you do when the story are working on starts to feel lacking and you have a bad case of shiny new ideas syndrome? First of all, don't fall for it. You'll never get anything done if you jumping from idea to idea.

So you said okay, but how do you stay focused on one idea when you may have so many coming into your head? Here's what I usually do if I have a totally new story idea, I write it down in a separate story Journal. Then I put the Journal away. That way I know the ideas written down and I won't forget it. Then when the project I'm working on is done, I can start working on a new idea.

Maybe for you is a different problem. Maybe the story has started to become boring. When that happens try to figure out why. Are things going with you nicely for your character? It might be time to add a little conflict. Also, you finding it hard to stay focused because you don't know when stories going then maybe it's time to go back to your research. I can't express us enough of how you have to want to read. Reading helps you stay inspired. On the other hand, if you having trouble staying focused because you lost total interest in the idea, then it might be time to start a new project. But if this is a reoccurring thing for you, like it was for me. Then take a step back and identify why. The reason why I was having trouble staying focused on a project, was the fact that I was wanting too many other distractions to get in the way. I complain about not having enough time but I wasn't using the time that I did have. For me, I found the strength of this is easier when I focus on one project. Also, I made plans about when I was going to write and I also explored certain times of the day to see what I write best. I also found that weekends were best for me because I'm not stressed out and tired from school . I also found that not worrying about the first draft helps me as well. The first draft is never meant to be perfect, is never meant to be the thing you turn into a publisher. It's just for getting your ideas down. Whenever I realize this and whenever I realized that editing was actually an easy process once you have the rough draft, it made it easier to focus on the story and my purpose for writing.

I also find that again having a writing partner really helps me staying focused. It helps me to have praise or criticism to motivate me. So maybe you're not staying focused because you're not motivated. If that's the case, have someone read your work asking that they liked it and what you can do to make it better. Maybe having trouble staying focused because running dry on ideas. Maybe reading a book doesn't necessarily help you. If that so just talks with friends about it, friends that like writing. Sometimes batting off ideas is a really good way to get ideas going again. And thus, it helps you stay focused.

The most important thing I wanted to take away from this chapter, is not to give into shiny new idea syndrome. Stick with your story and finish it. Here's a reason to stay focused even if none of these tips work for you. Finish the story to know you can finish it. Just to say that you did it. That's a really good feeling whenever you can so you finished something you started.

Here's some advice for staying focused in the moment. (Because I know when the family is watching sports it can be hard to concentrate) try to get yourself to a quiet place like your room. Try to eat or drink before writing. If you like music to try to turn on music with no lyrics and it. Classical music is good. Also, try to wear noise canceling headphones. Again it might be a good idea to use a timer to keep yourself on task and from getting distracted. I hope these tips help you stay focused.

Chapter 11

Writers block

Okay so were focusing on productivity, and I think there's one topic that we haven't discussed in detail but this whole book should help you to avoid it. In fact just to make sure you avoid it, I'm writing this whole chapter on it. The topic is writer's block. Yes, I know writer's block is the bane of creative writing existence. That's why working to solve it right now.

There are two main reasons for why people have writer's block. Let's look at the reasons. Maybe you went blank and you just don't know what happens next. When that happens it might be a good idea to go back your plotting. Start asking yourself what if questions, like what if my character did this or this? Make a bolded list of the questions, then try to answer them, until you know what you want to happen in the scene.

The next reason you might be having a right block, is the need for perfection. We all know that feeling of wanting to put the perfect sentence down. We all want to use the perfect words. We forget that our rough draft isn't supposed to be perfect. Here's what you do in those situations. Give yourself permission to write badly; do whatever you need you to get the story down. Use shallow words if needed. Guess what? You can fix it later. But you can't fix what doesn't exist. Please be aware that you may have to push the through the writing and make yourself write.

Maybe the reason you're experiencing writer's block. Is because you're not inspired. Look, writing isn't easy. But if you over exhaust yourself, you'll burn out. In these cases where you're just tired give yourself permission to take a break. Try to take a 30-minute break and then come   back to it. Also, continue reading look for inspiration everywhere. A book isn't going to be finished in a day.

So hopefully these tips help you to ask your writer's block. Hopefully, this whole book can guide you.

Other tips

Okay now and go over some other tips that I may have not got a chance to talk about yet. Some of my friends that are authors work in groups. If you're working in a group it can make a big writing project much easier but it also comes with its own challenges. First of all, a group is relying on you now so, don't slack on your part! The group will motivate you. Also be aware that you guys may butt heads as far as what you want to happen on the story. Please make sure to consider everyone's ideas.

I personally have never worked in a group before. So I can't really give too many tips on this other than these.

Secondly, I know I might have said this before but please be patient with yourself and don't procrastinate. Break the project up into little parts; try to do something with your book each day. That way working little by little and it doesn't seem like a big writing project.

And most of all have fun! Writing is supposed been enjoyable artistic experience. Be yourself, take advice from wherever you can and grow as a writer. That's probably the best advice anyone can

ever give you.

<u>Closure</u>

Well, I'm winding down to the end of this book. I'm glad to have shared this experience and advice for you. I hope this helps you; I learned so much on my journey to write this book. I hope that as you grow as a writer; you'll cherished experience, just as I am. Don't ever be afraid to write how you feel. That may seem silly but it took me a long time to understand that in the beginning. I wish you the best of luck in your writing journey. I'll be publish as many books as you want; rather it's just one or 1000. I'm glad you took the time to read this book. Seriously, I cannot thank you enough.

Good luck on the journey.

I did a lot of research during this project. On the next page is a works cited page. I couldn't have written this without those resources. Hopefully, you can find some resources that help you. Special thanks to the authors that wrote the resources. No copyright infringement intended. Thank you.

Works Cited

Brenda Miller. "A Braided Heart: Shaping The Lyric Essay."
Writing Creative Nonfiction. Story: Cincinnati, 2001.

On the Info Dump." *YouTube,* uploaded by bookishpixie, Nov. 24,
2015, \https://www.youtube.com/watch?v=O5TpuAqv3Vc.

"How To Write A Book In Less Than 24
Hours." *YouTube,* uploaded by Project Life Mastery, May 1, 2014,
https://www.youtube.com/watch?v=Oxfkkfc_79Y.

Edwards, Kim. "Icebergs, Glaciers, and Artic Dreams: Developing
Characters." *Creating Fiction*. Story: Cincinnati, 1999.

Judith Ortiz Cofer. "But Tell It Slant: From Poetry to Prose and

Back again." *Writing Creative Nonfiction*. Story: Cincinnati, 2001

.

Lan Samantha Chang. "Time and Order: The Art of Sequencing."

Creating Fiction. Story: Cincinnati, 1999. 137-144

Peck, Robert. *How to Write Fiction like a Pro*. Maupin House, 2006.

Terry Tempest Williams. "Why I Write." *Writing Creative*

Nonfiction. Story: Cincinnati, 2001.

Philip Gerard. "The Architecture of Light: Structuring the Novel and

Story Collection." *Creating Fiction*. Story: Cincinnati, 1999.

Writers Digest. Write Better, Get Published. 2016,

http://www.writersdigest.com/. Accessed 7 Dec. 2016.